Tiny

White Lion
Press

essentials of
monthly
committed
giving

To Ken, Marie, Joe and Charlie for your humour, values and zest for life.

To Ian, James and Marcia for all of the above too.

And in memory of Anatolia Mushaya and Tisa Chifunyise, heroes in the fight against AIDS.

White Lion
Press

Tiny

essentials of
monthly
committed
giving

by Harvey McKinnon

Published by
The White Lion Press Limited
Kermarquer
56310 Melrand
France

© 2006 Harvey McKinnon/The White Lion Press
Limited
ISBN-13: 978-0-9553993-0-5
ISBN-10: 0-9553993-0-0
All rights reserved

First printed 2006

Models: Charlie Burnett and Lucie Samson

Photography of 'Joe Charles' and 'twins' by
Adrian Taylor

Cover photography by Ken Burnett

Other photography: shark by Matilda Taylor;
'Helga' by Charlie Burnett; mask by Ken Burnett;
landscape and lighthouse by Ernest Muller

Design and print production by em associates

Printed and bound in the United Kingdom by
Bell & Bain Ltd

Contents

The author

Harvey McKinnon is one of North America's leading annual giving experts. He is the author of *Hidden Gold* (Bonus Books, Chicago) and co-author of *The Power of Giving* (www.thepowerofgiving.org).

Harvey has produced two best-selling training videos and an audio CD of his popular seminar, 'How Today's Rich Give', the first resource on the subject (Jossey-Bass, San Francisco). For a decade he also owned and ran a multi-award-winning television production company whose films have been aired on the BBC, CBC, PBS and in dozens of countries.

He has served on a wide variety of boards over the years including Oxfam, Greenpeace, The Brainerd Foundation and The Vancouver International Comedy Festival. He runs a successful direct response company, Harvey McKinnon Associates, which has served clients in many countries.

Harvey is a highly-rated speaker who regularly presents at many conferences throughout Canada and internationally. He knows 14,735 jokes and he can be reached at: info@harveymckinnon.com, or www.harveymckinnon.com.

Preface

This little book explains all you really need to know to justify, start, manage and benefit from monthly committed giving in your organisation.

Monthly giving is perfect for fundraisers because donors love it. They find it easy, convenient and affordable. It enables them to do a lot of good just by giving a small amount regularly that they will scarcely miss. A good monthly giving proposition will attract donors and keep them giving month after month for many years to come. Which explains why monthly giving is now viewed as the best, most cost-effective way of binding donors to a cause.

Vancouver-based Harvey McKinnon, author of this Tiny book, was one of the first fundraisers to spot monthly giving's potential and to bring it to the attention of fundraisers around the world. He deserves the description he was once given as the 'Pope of Monthly Giving'. Harvey has also directly influenced the health and viability of the voluntary sector on several continents. And he's helped his company's clients and other organisations to raise millions, even hundreds of millions, of dollars for their deserving causes.

The secrets of monthly committed giving are not rocket science. Neither are they complex, expensive or difficult to implement. They don't need huge amounts of management or large-scale staff resources. They don't require complicated technology or involve substantial risks.

This small book clearly describes the secrets of monthly giving, what they are and what they require. In an entertaining, readable yet practical way Harvey shares his insights, experience and wisdom. You can start benefiting from this simple yet superbly effective fundraising proposition in not much longer than the 60 minutes or so it will take you to read this book.

Enjoy.

Other books and resources by the author

Hidden Gold: How Monthly Giving Will Build Donor Loyalty, Boost Your Organization's Income and Increase Financial Stability, Bonus Books, Chicago 1999.

How Today's Rich Give, audio CD, Jossey-Bass, San Francisco 2003.

The Power of Giving: Creating Abundance in Your Home, at Work, and in Your Community, www.thepowerofgiving.org in conjunction with the Tides Canada Foundation, Vancouver 2005.

Acknowledgements

I want to express my gratitude to the many people I've worked with over the years: clients, co-workers and staff. You've given me the inspiration, time and resources to help build a lot of wonderful fundraising programmes – and learn a lot about monthly giving.

I'd also like to thank my good friends Ken and Marie Burnett for encouraging me to do this book and for editing it so well. And Rosemary Oliver, Nick Allen and James Julian, thank you for your helpful comments. I want to offer special thanks to my associate Carla Voss, who did everything one could do to help get this book finished.

And of course my thanks and love to my charming family – Marcia, James and Ian keep me happy and balanced.

Lastly I want to recognise all the people who pledge monthly to causes they believe in. You make the world a better place.

Praise for *Tiny Essentials of Monthly Committed Giving*

'This tasty morsel is a wonderful way to deliver valuable information that people will remember. As it turns out, Harvey is a master at storytelling along with being the master of monthly giving.'
Mark Anderson, CEO, Greening Australia SA, Australia.

'Everyone has time to read a tiny book and after you read this one, you'll be able to raise lots more money for your cause through setting up a monthly donor program. This is one of the best uses of an hour that I can think of.'
Rosemary Oliver, development director, Amnesty International, Canada.

'This tiny guide has given philanthropy a huge gift. McKinnon's entertaining style whilst sharing his formidable fundraising skills is in itself an act of selfless generosity.'
Lelei LeLaulu, president, Counterpart International; chairman, Foundation of the Peoples of the South Pacific, USA.

A happy accident

The last job I ever wanted was to be a fundraiser. Well, next to a lawyer, that is. Or perhaps a piano player in a house of ill repute.

I didn't like asking people for anything, much less money. I didn't like thinking about money all the time. It all seemed so, well, 'questionable'. Plato said, 'Death is not the worst than can happen to men [*sic*].' He was right. Having to ask someone for money is much worse.

But, like many things in life, you don't always get what you want. And I must admit, now that I've been a 'fundraiser' (I still prefer 'development officer') for five years, my attitude has changed.

Because, while I am a fairly accomplished piano player, I've decided to make fundraising my career.

My name is Joe Charles. And my story all started with a pair of blue-green eyes. Of course I was also inspired by the protection of our environment – a very serious issue. But truth be told, it was the blue-green eyes that started it all, that and… well, I'll tell you more later…

Luck and inspiration

I have a Master's degree in philosophy. Apparently it qualifies you for a lot of jobs where you get to wear a name badge and make the minimum wage.

Still, I've always felt that in addition to being a pseudo-intellectual, you actually have to work hard to get an MA in philosophy. Many commerce programmes graduate lazy students. But in philosophy you have to think hard – mostly about things like, 'Where on earth am I going to find a job?'

Which was how I ended up making telemarketing calls to sell burial plots:

1. I had to eat.

2. I had to pay the rent.

So calling strangers to convince them to pay for their grave and tombstone was a necessary evil.

At least I was philosophical about it and I'm sure my perspective helped me sell more tombstones. After all, philosophers make a career of thinking about life and death.

But as luck would have it, after a month of selling

burial plots, I was transferred to the fundraising section of the telemarketing company. They preferred to call it 'donor communications' but, let's face it, to the recipients of those irritating dinnertime calls, it is telemarketing.

Initially I resisted the transfer. It was easier to philosophise with people about death than to talk about money. But my manager made a good case: either switch departments or look for another job. So I became a fundraising caller for the Parks and Wilderness Society – PAWS to its donors.

Being a philosophy graduate, I spent most of my time reading dusty tomes in the library. The great outdoors, the wilderness, was not part of my 'natural environment'.

I was a city boy, only 25 and, despite the fact that I liked cycling, the wilderness was not something I could really relate to, that is, until we got our 'client briefing'.

As I discovered, clients can truly inspire us and improve our results by explaining how we help their cause. And I, like many of the other callers, did feel inspired.

Inspired callers mean more donors, more gifts and happier clients. Plus I got to put food in my fridge.

Two representatives from PAWS came to meet their callers. Gavin was an earnest, bald, 50-year-old who had spent a lifetime in the wilderness. As much as I could take in, he was in favour of trees, rivers and wildlife – and PAWS was a leading group protecting the same.

It's not that Gavin wasn't intensely passionate or interesting. Although, let me emphasise again that he was 'earnest'. It's just that his companion had – you guessed it – these incredible blue-green eyes that lit up when she described the opportunity we (the callers) had to protect wild spaces and wildlife. Oh, and her name was Helga.

Helga's passion was contagious and all of us set to the task of convincing PAWS donors to make monthly pledges to the cause. Her smile was like the sunrise and, well, I was young and single. I must confess, however, that asking people to spend their money was painful enough, but when it turned out that our job was to ask people to give money *every month*... That seemed quite ridiculous.

I thought that it was hard enough to ask someone for $25, but to ask for $25 a month? It seemed outrageously bold, like an overly optimistic fantasy.

And speaking of fantasies, Helga topped my list. I don't want to be too candid here, so let's just say she was the only goddess I'd ever met.

But, excuse me. This book is about raising money – raising money through monthly giving and raising an awful lot of it. Over the next seven chapters, I'll share everything I've discovered. And I believe that if you follow this path you'll reap great rewards.

So let us continue.

Motivation sometimes varies

I hated telemarketing scripts. But I do like to talk. And, in fact, given my philosophy degree, there was nothing I liked to do more than talk about big issues, intangibles, reason – even death.

That's why it didn't work out for me in the burial plot department. It seems I was too focused on the 'big' issues, such as why we are here and the meaning of life. There were a few complaints, though not nearly as many as you might think. Nevertheless, it was clear that fundraising was my last stop at the call centre.

What I learned was this: as much as I like to talk

about life and death, trying to sell a burial plot is difficult when you are only 25. Moreover, I didn't really care about what I was selling. And I felt that people should be cremated, as much as I enjoy wandering through graveyards.

But I digress. The transfer to the fundraising department taught me an important lesson. In order to be good at my job, I needed to care. And I

That's $300 a year and over a decade of giving adds up to the tidy little sum of $3,000.

learned to care about PAWS. Perhaps not for the most altruistic reasons (see Helga earlier) but I am concerned about our environment. A lot, actually. It's just that at this particular time I cared a lot more about making an impression on Helga.

I was incredibly lucky with my first fundraising call. I spoke to a PAWS donor who had been giving for five years, usually twice a year. A good 'prospect', I discovered. And when I asked her to make a monthly pledge, she agreed.

I've come to realise that when you want fledgling fundraisers to feel good about raising money, you need to make sure they succeed with their first ask.

Research shows that when two people gamble the one who wins the first time is much more likely to become addicted to gambling. Fundraising seems to be the same. It's an absolutely thrilling, endorphin-releasing experience when people say yes to your request for money. Conversely, it can be a real drag when people say no.

I'm sure my call was one of the worst in fundraising history, but my prospect was ready – a loyal donor who was practically begging to be asked to make a greater commitment.

Real value

Another great lesson: PAWS had never asked its donors to make a monthly pledge before. This meant I was the first to ask this wonderful donor who helped set me on a fun and rewarding career path. It was almost as if I was doing her a favour.

My donor (I felt like she was mine) agreed to give $25 a month. That's $300 a year and over a decade of giving adds up to the tidy little sum of $3,000. My $12-an-hour wage seemed like a pretty good investment for PAWS. Over the course of the next three hours, I recruited two more 'monthlies' and another $425 in single gifts from 10 donors who each declined to make a monthly pledge at that time.

My fellow callers recruited another 18 monthly donors. The resulting overall monthly gross for PAWS was $400. But the real value comes from the long-term giving. These 21 donors will probably give $30,000 to $60,000 to PAWS over time. Not to mention… well, we'll get to the real 'gold' in the chapter 'The long-term value is amazing'.

Helga never came back to the telemarketing company, much to my dismay. So after two months of raising what I calculated to be $160,000 in future value through monthly gifts for PAWS, I decided it was time to learn more about the environment.

With some trepidation, I wandered into the PAWS office one sunny Friday. I asked if there was a volunteer coordinator and was led down a long, messy hall covered in wilderness posters and a lot of dust. I wondered if maybe environmentalists didn't believe in keeping a clean office environment.

I entered a large room filled with recycled furniture (meaning it was old, probably free and, therefore, recycled). Tanis greeted me with a big smile and a face covered in multiple piercings. I thought that she had more metal on her than a war hero. Was I an overly conservative 25-year-old because of my philosophy degree? I don't know. But I'm certain that seven piercings *had* to hurt.

But I soon forgot my initial impression. Tanis was very warm and professional. I felt welcome. I was interviewed, I was given options. And I was re-inspired by her enthusiasm for PAWS.

As she showed me around the offices, I kept an eye out for Helga. She wasn't there. But my disappointment was countered by the nice people and the opportunity to (yes, it's a cliche) make a difference.

Tanis was delighted to hear about my telemarketing success and told many of the other volunteers and staff, so I was an instant celebrity.

After all, I was raising a lot of money for their cause.

That's when I realised on a deeper level that I was doing something really important. I still loved philosophy, but here was something practical. Something that was clearly tangible. And if I helped protect large wild spaces, I'd have a quiet place to go and contemplate Aristotle and Descartes.

Then she posed the question that would change my life forever.

Since I made my telemarketing calls later in the day, I decided to volunteer at PAWS for a few hours on most weekday mornings.

And then a week later, I met Helga again.

A life-changing question

She said she remembered me, so of course I blushed. She thanked me for becoming a volunteer and finding so many monthly donors.

Then she posed the question that would change my life forever.

'Would you become our expert?' Helga asked.

I think I blushed again, especially when I had to ask, 'Expert in…?'

I was sure she had just told me, but my brain had been preoccupied with thoughts of a more personal and intimate nature.

Nevertheless, she said politely, 'An expert on monthly giving.'

I guess I looked a little stunned, so she elaborated.

'You already know as much as any of the PAWS staff and you've recruited more monthly donors than anyone else. And you're a volunteer and, well, we really need to raise more money.'

'But', I stammered, 'I don't like asking for money. I mean I love what PAWS does, but I only call people because I need a job. Plus, I'm especially uncomfortable asking for money face to face.'

'That's okay. And you don't have to ask. We just want you to do research. You've probably done lots of that.'

Well, if you want research on existentialism I'm your guy, but I didn't know anything about fundraising research.

'I'll make it easy for you. Have you heard of Google?' she smiled.

Now, it could have been a 'what are you, an idiot?' kind of smile, but it felt like a kind smile, for a reluctant fundraising researcher. Plus, I think the fact that the smile also came with a sparkle in her eyes made me say, 'of course'.

'Also', she said, 'I know a few people who work at other charities. I could arrange for you to talk to the fundraisers about what they do. Then, when you think you've gathered enough information, summarise it for me in a report.'

So I started that morning. I lined up three interviews and I was on my way.

Key learning points

It's important to cultivate passion for your cause amongst your staff and volunteers – there lies the secret of fundraising success.

Inspired fundraisers mean more donors and more gifts.

Make sure that the first time a staff member or volunteer asks for a donation, the donor is likely to say 'yes'. This builds confidence and lays the groundwork for future success.

Even if your organisation doesn't have a monthly donor programme yet, almost certainly you already have single gift donors who are just waiting to be asked to make a greater commitment.

Passion is the key to success

Helga's friend at the Stephen Lewis Foundation was Tisa Mushaya. (Stephen Lewis was a United Nations special envoy for HIV/AIDS in Africa; he is a former deputy director of UNICEF and is a hero in the fight against AIDS.) She greeted me with a warm smile and an energy I wish I could bottle.

Helga had told me that Tisa was an AIDS activist in Southern Africa who had fled her country because of its political and social instability.

And, just like her life back home in Africa, Tisa

was still working for her people, only this time from afar.

Tisa ushered me into her office. The walls had three AIDS prevention posters. The shelves were overflowing with books and files and there were a couple of beautiful African carvings. As we sat down she asked how she could help me and I knew it was something she'd said often – and meant it every time.

The important part

'Helga said you could help me learn about fundraising.'

'Isn't Helga wonderful!' she exclaimed.

'I don't really know her that well', I replied, 'although I'd like to get to know her better.

'She says that you have a lot of monthly donors. PAWS needs to get a lot more of them and, according to Helga, you are an expert in this area.'

'I'm not too bad', Tisa demurred, 'but would you like to know why I choose to do this kind of work? That's the important part.'

'Sure', I said.

'I do what I do because I want to raise money for people with AIDS. My husband died from AIDS. I've seen many wonderful human beings die because of ignorance, fear and poverty. And in my heart, I believe we can stop this. I don't know if you've ever watched someone die. But when they die from AIDS, they suffer dreadfully and, to add to the tragedy, most people leave children behind. There are so many orphans and even many babies born with AIDS.

'I've seen this in my country and in others as well', Tisa continued, 'and I have to do what I can. It's why I have passion. And it's why I'm not afraid to ask for money, because I know that every dollar, pound, or euro helps so much.

'I'll tell you everything I can to help you and I think the best way to start would be to tell you how our monthly donors help. May I do that?'

'Sure', I said, 'I'm here to learn everything I can.'

'Okay', she enthused, 'our incredibly committed and generous monthly supporters save lives. It's that simple. Their monthly gifts go to AIDS education and prevention, to care for AIDS orphans and to self-help projects for teenagers and adults living with HIV and AIDS. And, as you probably know, money goes an incredibly long way in Africa.'

Then she smiled, 'But really, the best way to learn about monthly giving is to become a monthly donor yourself. So, let me ask you: will you join our monthly donor programme to help people with AIDS in Africa?'

Tisa was now deadly serious. She looked me directly in the eye. It really didn't take long for me to reply, 'Yes, I'd like to, but I only make $450 a week doing telemarketing. Would $10 a month be okay?'

The beaming smile returned to her face.

'You are a kind man. And that's how you ask someone for a monthly gift. You describe the need. You tell people how their gift will help. You let them know why you are passionate about the work. Passion is contagious. People want to feel it. They want to experience what is best about being human; they need to feel that they are helping others. Working together to solve problems builds a community and connections. People give for emotional reasons and a good fundraiser taps into their desire to make a difference, to stop suffering, to give love.'

Questions and answers

Tisa grinned mischievously, 'And then the most important thing is…'

I returned her gaze, wide-eyed, clueless as to what that might be.

She leaned toward me, spread her hands on her desk and said, 'You have to remember to *ask*.'

Tisa went on to explain that the number one reason why people don't give is because *no one has asked them*.

I thought, well, that's easy for her to say because she's comfortable about asking. I, on the other hand, was terrified.

'I can see you don't feel comfortable asking for money', Tisa observed. 'Most people don't. Really, it's a learned skill.'

She paused, tilted her head slightly, and asked, 'Have you ever asked a woman out?'

'Well…', I stammered, 'sort of.'

'That's actually much harder to do than to ask for a donation', Tisa said. 'If she says no, you might feel personally rejected – even if there is a perfectly good reason for it, which might have nothing to do with whether or not she likes you.'

I felt my blood pressure rise. Was this some sort of Zimbabwean mind-reading trick? She couldn't possibly know how I felt about Helga, could she?

'So, just like asking for a date, asking for money is a bit of a risk. But when people say no, they aren't actually rejecting you.'

She regarded me carefully and said, 'You know, I think you'll get the hang of it. The key is that if you don't ask, you can never get what you want.'

A hint of mischief returned to Tisa's face and I was pretty certain that she had been referring to Helga. I felt my cheeks flush with embarrassment (obviously I needed to get outdoors more often to develop a tan to cover the overly sensitive blood vessels in my face). But – back to fundraising.

'So again, let me repeat: it is important to remember that if people say no, they aren't rejecting you, or even your cause', Tisa continued. 'They might have a wonderful reason. And whatever that reason is, it's their right to say no. You should never take it personally.

'Remember, when it comes to fundraising, no might mean that you haven't given donors enough information, or discovered what they care about, or resolved a possible objection that they might have.

'That's why when someone says no, you ask for a reason. Then you listen to him or her carefully and prove that you listened by restating the objection. Then, if you can, you put her concerns to rest and – *ask again*.'

'The key is that if you don't ask, you can never get what you want.'

Tisa must have noticed the look on my face, which was probably an 'I'm-not-sure-I-get-it' look.

'Here – let me give you an example. I want you to give me a reason why someone might not make a monthly pledge.'

'They live on a telemarketer's salary?' I offered tentatively.

Tisa exploded with laughter. 'I can easily overcome that excuse in a matter of seconds. The reality is that when people feel moved, they will give. I've seen incredibly poor people be very generous with what they have. That is not the case with everyone of course; some people try to hang onto everything they ever get. But most people are very giving and I've often been truly touched by the generosity of people who have very little. I've seen women who barely get one meal a day share their food with people dying from AIDS. It's both heartbreaking and inspiring. In the West we are so rich with money. But we need to be richer with compassion.'

As her words sank in, I realised that she had obliterated my excuse in 30 seconds flat.

'So really, money isn't the core issue, is it?'

'So really, money isn't the core issue, is it?'

Tisa shook her head wisely. 'Research shows that people with lower incomes tend to give a higher percentage of their incomes to charities. And of course, they have less money to share in the first place. So give me another excuse.'

'Uhh, I've had a big tax bill (not likely, given my salary) and it'll take me six months to cover it', I said.

'My response would be, "I'm sorry to hear that and I can understand how that could be difficult." This is an example of reflecting back with empathy – but it has to be genuine on your part. Then I'd say, "but your past support shows how much you care about this cause and since you know your monthly pledge will literally save lives and prevent babies from getting AIDS, let me ask you this: when you are finished paying your tax bill in, say, six months and are used to living on less, would you join then? I know you are moved by this cause and I know you want to help so, six months from now, would you consider committing yourself to give just $1 a day?" '

That could work, I thought. She clearly was empathetic and understood the person's situation. And she had found a creative solution.

'What about this?' I ventured. 'I'm worried about my money being stolen. I hear about that a lot with overseas charities. How do I know my money won't be wasted?'

'That is a very valid concern', Tisa said. 'Yes, aid does go missing, although that tends to happen when donations go from government-to-government but not so much with a non-governmental organisation like ours. And, like all donors, I want to make every penny have the maximum impact. Since I personally have seen how great the need is, I have a choice. I can ignore the suffering, or I can choose to do my best to protect our donors' money – including mine! So that's what we do. We have staff on the ground to make sure our assistance goes directly to the people who need it. We know that our aid does reach people. And we know that development projects – training, education and health clinics – are safer than massive food aid projects, which can be tempting to unscrupulous individuals.

'Our goal is to treat every donor's money like it was our own. That way we work hard to make sure it is well spent. I've seen many of these projects myself. I've seen the grateful looks in people's eyes and I've seen the difference that good people like you make.

So I ask you again, will you give $1 a day to help our AIDS work?'

Understanding and experience

Wow! She went really easy on me, I thought. With her skills, she very easily could have had me giving $30 a month. It wasn't until later that I realised how Tisa had quickly assessed my giving ability based on my age and income. She wanted me to give at a level that wouldn't be unmanageable or unrealistic. She knew that if I felt financially overwhelmed, I'd soon quit. And she also knew that my real value as a donor was long term. Tisa's experience told her that as I age and my income increases, I might give much more – as long as her organisation manages to keep me inspired about how my donations make a difference.

I had started to enjoy this exercise and came up with eight more objections. Tisa handled them all beautifully, except for one. The one she couldn't handle was…

Ahh, but this book is small (tiny, actually) and there's not much room. You'll have to visit the monthly giving guru's website, www.harveymckinnon.com, to find the one and only objection not even Tisa could counteract. I know it'll be worth your time, because there is a great deal of other information on monthly giving there for you. I was hoping to interview Harvey for this book, but unfortunately he was too busy playing Sudoku on his computer, or at least that's what his executive assistant told me.

Key learning points

People give for emotional reasons. Inspire emotion and people will make a commitment.

The number one reason people don't donate to a cause is: they haven't been asked. The number one reason why people neglect to join a monthly donor programme is the same: they haven't been asked.

It's important to train any monthly giving solicitors to deal with objections by listening carefully, restating the objection, then dealing with it. Many objections are simply ways of saying 'I'm not convinced'.

Obstacles

After just one interview, I had already joined my first monthly giving programme. I reckoned that if the next two interviews went like the one with Tisa, I'd soon be a hungry man.

But, as it turned out, the second interview didn't cost me any money, although it did cost me time. At first I felt like I'd learned nothing. It was only later that I grasped the real lessons.

I knocked on Beatrice Snodgrass's office door at 9:46 a.m.

'You're late!' were her first admonishing words – after all, a minute's a minute when you're an important executive at the Institute for Chronic Pain.

Mrs Snodgrass could not be described as a soothing personality. I was nervous as soon as I saw her. I instantly pictured her as a shark in a pool – and myself as the lone swimmer floating in the middle.

But in spite of my nervousness, I explained my mission. And I reminded her that a friend of Helga's father, Mr Little (one of her biggest donors), had suggested that I talk to her.

This seemed to placate her, at least long enough for her to offer me a seat. I wouldn't exactly say that she became friendly, but at least I stopped picturing her circling me as a potential meal. And so the interview began.

'Monthly donors?' she said with noticeable disdain. 'We've got a few. Bit of a nuisance really, because we have to mail them a notice each month and that's a real headache. Our staff are very busy and sometimes don't get the bills out on time. Plus the donors don't always do what they say they will. They say they'll give 12 times a year, but the average is only about nine or 10 times. That's the problem with people today – no commitment', she grumbled.

Well, to save you, the reader, from the squirming agony that I endured, let me summarise the rest of the 45-minute lecture I received. I did manage to get in about three questions during that time but, since they weren't really answered, I'll spare you the details.

Basically, Mrs Snodgrass didn't care much about monthly donors: 'small time, small gifts' is what she said. Her attitude was to pay attention only to the potentially big donors. Also, because her charity only sent out monthly reminder notices by mail, the fulfilment rate was about 80 per cent and those notices were expensive to send out. The number of monthly donors who dropped out of the programme each year was about 30 per cent. And it was clear that Mrs Snodgrass saw these low-dollar donors as a burden.

'... and that accounts for almost all of our donors.'

I tried to point out that I gave my new monthly gift through automatic bank deductions, but her curt response was, 'People don't like that technology, especially those who are over 50 – and that accounts for almost all of our donors.'

I took note of the absence of a computer in her office, but at least she had a phone.

So ultimately, Mrs Snodgrass had three core reasons why she wasn't interested in developing the Institute for Chronic Pain's monthly giving programme:

1. The donations were too small.

2. It was too much work.

3. Her health charity's donors were too old.

Her steadfastness, her position of authority and the

fact that she worked for a large charity made me pause for a few minutes after I stumbled out of her office. Was I just being swept up in the charm and enthusiasm of Helga and Tisa? Was Mrs Snodgrass, the senior executive with the most experience, the wise one?

Time did tell. And the lessons I learned from Mrs Snodgrass became clear after talking to Ian James, the monthly giving specialist at World First.

Key learning points

Many nonprofit staff and board members fear change, even if the change is clearly beneficial. Those who are particularly risk-averse will miss out on wonderful opportunities and may even endanger the long-term stability of their organisation.

Collecting monthly gifts by cheque is the most costly and least effective method. You need to implement a strategy to convert cheque donors to electronic (automatic) giving.

It's easy to make assumptions

about donors that are not always accurate.

Just because people have a strong position on an issue does not mean they are right.

It is important to examine how a monthly donor programme is implemented; what resources are allocated to it and to calculate the long-term value of a monthly donor. This forms the basis of an intelligent allocation of resources.

The long-term value is amazing

Ian James was a boyish, 30-something-year-old, mature to me but a baby compared with Mrs Snodgrass. He ushered me into a large, active office where dozens of people were working at computers and many more were milling about, on the phone, in small discussion groups and in meeting rooms.

When I told him about the newly discovered objections to monthly giving, drilled into my head by the power of Mrs Snodgrass, all he could do was laugh. That felt good and his explanation was entertaining.

'First', he said, 'the fundraising world is full of

Snodgrasses. We should coin that term and have it refer to people who believe the only thing that should ever change is their underwear. Seriously, they do so much damage to charities. I'll bet she's never heard of the internet and she thinks a blog is a horror movie.

'People like her do a terrible disservice to good causes', Ian explained. 'They are stuck with a mindset that doesn't look at any options other than the traditional ones – major gifts, grants and, maybe, direct mail. All of these are great ways to make lots of money, but there are other methods that can raise a fortune for a good cause.

'I think their problem is fear of change', Ian continued. 'They won't embrace it, learn from it. And frankly, monthly giving isn't even all that new. Many groups have been doing it for decades. World First has branches in 30 countries around the world and altogether has built up to about 500,000 monthly donors. And we're not very large compared to some other global charities. Today those 500,000 monthly donors give an average of $20 a month each. That's roughly $10 million each and every month. And many of these donors will give for the rest of their lives because their gifts are transferred electronically.'

Even if I hadn't been making just $450 a week as a telemarketer, $10 million each month would still have seemed like an awful lot of money; $120 million in a year seemed like an incredible amount.

Myths

'Now – let me explode some of Mrs Snodgrass's beliefs.' Ian grinned and cleared this throat with mock officiousness. 'First of all, it's a myth that it's too much work. When I started here at the national office, we had one person managing 7,000 monthly donors. This included donor interactions ranging from change of address requests to handling extra gifts to mailing newsletters. And the programme brought in $2 million a year! Now two people manage 25,000 donors quite efficiently and still have lots of time to do other work. Automatic transfers are much easier and cheaper to process than cheque donations, which saves us a significant amount of staff time.'

'That's amazing', I said. 'I can't believe that 25,000 donors can be looked after so easily.'

Ian smiled and continued, 'It's a lot easier than most people think. And the return on investment is great. You told me that Mrs Snodgrass thinks monthly donations are too small to matter. Well, she's forgetting the key factor: if a donor gives you $15 a month, which is $180 a year, and you have just 1,000 of these donors, this adds up to $180,000. It's not necessary to build a massive donor base in order to make this worthwhile.'

'Maybe I should send Mrs Snodgrass my notes', I interjected.

'No kidding', Ian laughed. 'You know, around the world Greenpeace now has an annual income of around US$ 200 million, most of which comes from upwards of two million regular givers. Keep in mind that in any year an average monthly donor will give two to three times as much as a donor who only gives once a year. When you convert annual donors to monthly donors, you can significantly increase your income without actually growing your donor base. Monthly donors also tend to be much more loyal and will most likely stay on your donor list for many, many years.

'An important factor is how nonprofits treat their donors.'

Method of recruitment matters

'The way that a donor is recruited makes an even bigger difference to how long they will keep giving', Ian explained. 'Basically, direct mail donors stay the longest. Donors recruited by telemarketing are pretty steadfast as well, but the biggest annual drop-off rates come from face-to-face recruitment and direct response television ads. That said, the drop-off rates vary quite widely. An important factor is how nonprofits treat their donors. For example, they need to thank their donors promptly, keep them inspired about the cause and to communicate effectively through their newsletters and websites.'

'What about the drop-off rate for online recruitment?' I enquired.

'So far World First has done well with online donors, but we just don't have the long-term tracking studies that will tell us precisely how loyal they are', Ian answered. 'However, things look good so far, but I do know some organisations that direct television donors to their websites and they do experience a higher drop-off rate than us.'

Age isn't important

I contemplated this for a moment and then asked, 'What about a donor's age? Why do you think Mrs Snodgrass is convinced that her organisation's donors are "too old" to be interested?'

Ian sighed gently. 'I've often heard people say that their donors are "too old" and won't join a monthly giving programme. But a friend of mine works for a charity whose average donor is 72 years old. And thousands of these donors give monthly. For elderly donors, automatic deductions are convenient. Automatic payments for everything from the monthly gas and electricity bills to newspaper subscriptions and rent or mortgage payments are growing at a rapid rate, especially among older people. And religious causes, whose donor bases are made up mostly of senior citizens, pioneered monthly giving.'

He paused for a moment to let this sink in. 'Now', Ian continued, 'the reality is that no organisation will be able to get 100 per cent of its donors on a monthly giving programme. The key is being able to get five to 30 per cent of your donors to give monthly. This can easily increase a donor's long-term value 10 to 20 fold. In some cases, especially in Europe where monthly giving has been promoted for decades, it's often 30 to 50 times more value per donor. For this reason, some groups only ask for monthly pledges and might even discourage single gifts. The way to measure the success of a fundraising programme is to evaluate the initial cost of acquiring a new donor and then to track carefully how long they stay on your file – i.e. that they continue to donate.'

Another important thing

I could tell Ian was on a roll. He was truly in his element and his passion for the profession really showed. He barely paused for a breath before continuing.

'Another important thing to think about is: can your organisation tie a monthly amount to an appealing area? For example, the great proposition in monthly giving programmes is child sponsorship. Organisations that offer child sponsorships make people feel like they are directly connected to the children. There's probably nothing more appealing than that. The exception to the five to 30 per cent rule would be child sponsorship nonprofits, because they usually have a minimum of 50 per cent of donors giving monthly.' (See the key learning points at the end of this chapter for an explanation of this principle.)

'Although', he added, 'some animal charities also attract an enormous number of monthly donors.

Children and animals have a remarkable way of evoking a deep emotional response, which compels a lot of people to make a regular commitment. I'm sure you know that inspiring people is critically important. If people feel inspired they will, in fact, give you more money. But if they feel like they're being sold to they aren't likely to give you their money. It's the same thing when you go into a car dealership.'

I looked at him quizzically.

'Well', Ian explained, 'when you go to buy a car and someone is friendly, open and trustworthy you're much more likely to buy from him – it usually is a him – than from someone who is obviously trying to sell you something by any means necessary. So, what I'm trying to say is, it's very important to be genuine and thoughtful every time you communicate with donors and potential donors.

A basic fundraising principle… or two

'Let me give you another pointer on communication – it's important to link the donor with the solution. So, instead of saying "we, the organisation, will solve this problem", you should communicate to donors that *they* are the ones who solve the problem by making a donation.'

'What about PAWS?' I enquired eagerly. 'Do you think it would be a good idea to tie a monthly amount to a wilderness area, or maybe an animal habitat? For example, what if PAWS could say that for every $30, one hectare of forest will be protected?'

'Exactly!' Ian was clearly pleased. 'That's a quick understanding of a basic fundraising principle.

'Here's another one for you', he said excitedly. 'All research shows that longevity of giving is usually the greatest predictor of a donor's willingness to leave a legacy. Countless nonprofits have found that it is not the size of the annual gift that is the most important factor, but years of giving. The one method of fundraising that's most likely to renew donors for multiple years is…' Ian paused dramatically.

'This is how you build a closer relationship.'

'Monthly giving?' I guessed.

'Right again. And people who give monthly are even better legacy prospects than people who give single gifts for multiple years', Ian explained. 'Now, it could be that they are self-selecting, meaning that donors who join a monthly giving programme are already truly committed to your cause. I'm sure that this is true, but I also think that you build better relationships with donors who join a programme. Your communication with them doesn't always have to focus on asking for more money. You can report back to them on how their gifts were spent and you can honour them for their ongoing generosity. This is how you build a closer relationship.'

I nodded to show that I understood, not wanting to interrupt Ian's train of thought.

Real gold

'I believe that people who include charities in their wills are most likely to choose the one – or ones – that they've given to for the greatest amount of time. Monthly giving makes it easy for people to give year after year', Ian said. 'This is the real gold – which needs to be added to the sum of their monthly gifts. It often gets counted under planned or major gifts, but the initial relationship and the interaction over the years usually comes from the monthly giving relationship. Organisations need to factor this in when they calculate long-term value. And the values depend greatly on the organisation and their marketing skills and resources.'

I could easily tell that Ian was excited because he was grinning and wringing his hands enthusiastically.

I thought, 'PAWS is going to be interested in the potential gold mine of planned giving and monthly donors.'

Ian went on to give me a full hour of great tips that I later summarised for Helga in a memo called 'the top 43 monthly giving fundraising tips' (see page 47).

Finally, Ian said that he would be needed in another meeting shortly. But before we parted, he said, 'Let me give you just a few pointers about monthly giving clubs. These are a great way to make donors really feel like they truly belong to your organisation – that their contribution is recognised and valued. A monthly giving club is part of the integrated marketing strategy that every organisation should have, even though most don't. All nonprofits need to plan how they will promote their monthly giving club: by mail, online, or in newsletters. In many cases the phone, face-to-face fundraising in all its forms, or special events are a key part of an organisation's strategy for monthly donor recruitment and communication. The bottom line is that it's important to *evaluate each method and test its effectiveness.*'

I nodded to signal that I understood and asked Ian if I might be able to call him if I had any more questions. He kindly agreed, not knowing that I felt as though I still had about a thousand questions.

Key learning points

Donors are rarely too old for monthly giving programmes. In fact, many older donors like automatic transfer plans because it's convenient for them and they still get to help the causes they love.

When donors join a monthly giving programme, they give for

many years. Many will give monthly for the rest of their lives.

The time and money that it takes to manage a monthly donor programme is small compared to managing a similar number of donors who give single gifts. Monthly donors give more, while saving you money.

Monthly donors recruited by direct mail are almost always the most valuable over the long term.

Your organisation can expect to ultimately convert five to 30 per cent of your active donor base to monthly status. For some organisations it could be much more. Your success depends on your offer, your investment, your mission and your skills.

It is critical to analyse the long-term value of a monthly donor by the method of recruitment (mail, face to face, phone, etc). When you do this calculation make sure you factor in the cost of recruitment, as well as the cost to maintain the donor in the programme.

Small things can have a big cumulative impact if there are enough of them (e.g. mosquitoes).

Highly personal or chugging?

My mind was buzzing as I left the World First office. I'd visited three fundraisers and received three vastly different perspectives. But I felt like I'd collected what I needed for Helga, er, I mean PAWS.

Now, I thought to myself, I'll just put all the information into the context of Plato on commitment, Socrates on compassion and Aristotle on truth – and I'll have a stellar report. But, on reflection, I decided it would be better to leave out the dead philosopher stuff and stick to the facts.

I stopped at a coffee shop to start my report when I

noticed a person whom I'd always previously avoided. He wasn't exactly a homeless guy asking for change, but in my mind he was not far off.

No, he wasn't a prostitute or a 'street person'. He was a fundraiser – someone who was recruiting people to monthly committed giving. I, of course, had seen these people around, but always walked straight past. This was particularly easy for me because these people focused on attracting the attention of pedestrians who appeared to have money. I guess you could say it was a case of mutual lack of interest.

But I decided that this might be a golden opportunity to conduct some field research. So I grabbed a coffee and took it to an outside table within earshot of the solicitor and started observing.

Field notes from a coffee shop

First, I noticed that the solicitor had a partner. She was positioned not far from the subject I will call Daryl. I'll call her Daryl 2. Why, you might ask? Because he looked like an old friend named, well, Daryl and she looked like a young Daryl Hannah. This is probably why she had a number of young men interested in her monthly donor programme, while Daryl 1 kept trying to stop passers-by with less success. Although he did seem to talk to more women than men.

One of the things that I noticed immediately was startling: if I thought people were rude to telemarketers, they are much harder on people who try to recruit them as monthly donors on the street. I couldn't always hear their opening lines, but the Daryls smiled at virtually every passer-by and tried to engage each of them in conversation. They looked professional in the sense that they were wearing jackets that identified them as representatives of the charity. They each had a photo ID card around their neck (which I am sure was there because it lends credibility). Both Daryls were holding binders, which signalled to passers-by that they weren't asking for spare change.

... it seemed like a good way to get a large number of people to sign up in a short period of time.

I was surprised to overhear that people were given a gift when they signed up for $20 or more a month. I now know that this is referred to in fundraising jargon as a 'premium', or in the UK an 'incentive'. This particular charity was offering T-shirts to people who signed up at this amount or more. (This was unusual; I later learned that it is rare to use premiums in face-to-face fundraising. They are used most often in television ads to recruit monthly donors.)

During my two hours of anthropological observation I consumed four coffees. And among the things I learned is that after four coffees your hand shakes when you write. My second observation was that each of the Daryls appeared to recruit one donor, both of whom, like the Daryls, appeared to be in their twenties. In fact, the fundraisers clearly put more energy into talking to younger people. This made me think that there might be an age factor in whom they felt comfortable talking to – and also who was willing to talk to them. I subsequently learned that the better canvassers also look for social and visual 'clues' to determine if someone might be a better prospect. It could be a friendly or happy face. Or, for example, an environmental recruiter could be looking for an eco-friendly T-shirt, a canvas bag for groceries, a jacket logo from an environmentally friendly company and so on.

I calculated that by recruiting even one new $20 monthly donor in two hours, the Daryls would be raising far more than they were getting paid ($240 a year against maybe $10 to $20 an hour).

I thought back to what Ian had told me – that donors who are recruited face to face don't stay as long as donors recruited by other methods. But, based on my observation of the Daryls, it seemed like a good way to get a large number of people to sign up in a short period of time.

Eventually, after an hour of 'field research', I had to abandon my post because I was becoming very jittery after so much coffee. Since that day, I have learned a lot more about face-to-face recruitment by talking to people who are solicitors.

Disadvantages

What became clear to me through my research is that a lot of charities recruit a significant number of donors to their monthly giving programmes either by street soliciting or by knocking on doors. And if a charity uses paid canvassers, it's only cost-effective when donors are recruited to a monthly programme. As Ian told me, there are many advantages to using face-to-face methods, but there are also some substantial disadvantages.

... and make a huge difference to the long-term value of the entire fundraising programme.

The first major drawback is that many face-to-face campaigns have drop-off rates that are much higher than other methods of recruitment. For instance, attrition in the first year can range from about 20 per cent to 33 per cent. A further 15 per cent to 30 per cent drop off is common in the second year. When donors have been giving for two years the drop-off rate improves. But organisations must track this carefully to ensure they are getting value. An extra 10 per cent drop off each year makes a phenomenal difference in lifetime value for the original group that was recruited. My subsequent research shows that the drop-off rate can be influenced by how the charity treats donors once they become 'members'. So, a good quality donor communication programme will help to reduce the rate of attrition and make a huge difference to the long-term value of the entire fundraising programme.

The second drawback is that street solicitors might, in fact, damage the reputation of a credible organisation. I've heard that if you walk through certain parts of London you can be surrounded by street solicitors from several charities. On some days it's hard to walk two blocks without being harassed for money. Apparently, the problem has become so bad that the English press has coined the term 'chuggers' – charity muggers – to describe street solicitors. In fact, the head of one of Britain's leading charities was quoted in the press as saying that he realises that the practice is now damaging his charity's reputation, even though it has recruited tens of thousands of monthly donors through this method.

Indeed, amongst all the advice that Ian offered me was: when a particular place becomes saturated with face-to-face solicitation, not only will you be less likely to be successful at it, but you're also more likely to damage the reputation of your organisation. However, in North America relatively few towns or cities, if any, have become saturated by this form of fundraising. There might be areas where this has reached the levels seen in some European centres, but these would be the exception.

Nevertheless, face-to-face solicitation is a method that well-known 'brand name' charities should at least test, because of its enormous potential for acquiring new monthly donors. And, like all other forms of fundraising, if an organisation has a highly recognisable name and logo it has a huge advantage when approaching people on the street. Most people will already be familiar with the charity's work and will be far more likely to engage in conversation. This is, of course, the key to starting the process of signing up monthly donors.

Key learning points

Although undoubtedly financially successful, recruitment of monthly donors through face-to-face interaction has led to intense competition amongst charities in the UK and other parts of Europe, as well as alienating large numbers of potential donors – thus hurting many charities.

New or undeveloped markets still have significant potential for face-to-face recruitment. If face to face is done well and the nonprofit has a good

communications programme
for the people they recruit,
then it can be a worthwhile
investment.

Recognisable brand names give
an enormous advantage to
organisations using face-to-face
methods.

MEMORANDUM

TO: Helga

RE: The top 43 monthly giving fundraising tips

FROM: Joe

_____

1.   When a donor converts from single gifts to monthly giving, his or her lifetime value increases (on average) from eight to 30 times.

2.   Monthly donors demonstrate, through their loyalty and regular commitment, that they are excellent planned giving prospects.

3.   It is far better to recruit monthly donors to give electronically by direct debit (automatic funds transfer from a bank account), or by credit card. Donors who give by cheque have a higher attrition rate and fulfil fewer monthly pledges than donors who give by electronic means.

4.   To increase the longevity of giving, work hard to convert cheque or credit card donors to electronic funds transfer (EFT).

5.   EFT, or direct debit, is generally preferable to credit card deductions. The attrition rate is higher when credit cards are used because they expire, people cancel them, change them, exceed their limits, or lose them. All of these factors can result in lower lifetime values for these donors.

6.   Regular, ongoing and systematic promotion of monthly giving is the key to building a file (donor database).

7.   Testing what works (and doesn't work) with your conversion programme is essential.

8.   It's effective to invite new donors to join a monthly giving programme two to four months after their initial gift.

9.   Donors who give two or more gifts in a year are good prospects for a monthly giving invitation.

10. Using premiums can be a cost-effective way to recruit new monthly donors and can be used to encourage a higher initial monthly amount.

11. You should ask monthly donors to consider upgrading their monthly payment at least once, possibly twice, a year – the

second time as a reminder to the initial request. Generally speaking, a letter should be used for the first upgrade request because it is usually more cost-effective than a phone call.

12.   Most charities find that the greatest lifetime value for monthly donors comes from those who are recruited by direct mail.

13.   Younger donors convert to monthly giving most often through face-to-face solicitation. However, attrition rates can be quite high for this method. It is critical to track attrition rates (and costs) carefully.

14.   Direct response television (DRTV) can be an excellent way to recruit monthly donors. But there are many conditions that must be met: your organisation needs a brand name, you need to make people cry and you need to motivate them to pick up the phone. Also, you need creativity, the right time slot and, generally, you require a lot of investment money.

15.   Breaking down the monthly pledge into a daily cost helps to show people how a small amount of money adds up to a world of difference. Just 50 cents a day is $15 a month, or $180 a year, or $1,800 over a

decade. But it's only 50 cents a day.

16.   Monthly donors will be your best-responding segment when you have an emergency fundraising appeal.

17.   If your organisation is in a market where there is little face-to-face recruitment, you will do much better than you would in a market where the public is fed up with constant 'harassment'. In saturated markets, you risk being labelled a 'chugger' and you risk damaging your organisation's reputation.

18.   Making telemarketing calls to former and dormant donors (no gifts for three or more years) can be worthwhile. If you do telemarketing, test these groups for their response rates.

19.   Donors like the convenience of monthly giving – mention it in your recruitment invitations.

20.   Monthly donors are an excellent source of planned giving prospects. Make sure you add their names to your planned giving initiatives and mention planned giving to your monthly donors at appropriate times in letters or special newsletters.

21.   The members of staff responsible for issuing receipts and fielding calls from donors are very important to a successful programme. The 'service' they give to donors makes a significant difference in the longevity of giving, especially with less committed 'new' donors recruited directly to monthly giving from face-to-face and DRTV.

22.   It is critically important to analyse your return on investment (ROI) for all fundraising initiatives, particularly monthly giving. You need to evaluate ROI by source (e.g. direct mail versus telemarketing). This will tell you how much it is worth investing to acquire a new donor. The method of recruitment is a key factor in determining a donor's lifetime value.

23.   Your website can recruit good monthly donors. Since people who join through your website are taking the initiative by seeking you out, they will probably have a longer history of giving than donors you have to actively recruit.

24.   The key to recruiting monthly donors through your website is to follow the basic rules of good communication: great copy (content), clean design and emotional and

logical reasons to join your monthly giving programme. Your website must be easy to read and navigate.

25.   Recruitment through your website is highly dependent on traffic. You can have the best monthly giving proposition and the best website in the world, but if people can't find it, or don't come back for repeat visits you'll miss out on all of these potential monthly donors.

26.   Research shows that donors who support multiple charities and give in excess of $1,000 per year are excellent monthly giving prospects (especially when recruited through the mail or telephone). There is usually a correlation with religious affiliation as well.

27.   Donors recruited by DRTV and face-to-face methods fit a different profile than other donors. Compared to those recruited through direct mail and the telephone, these donors tend to be younger, give less to charity and change addresses more often.

28.   Never take your monthly donors for granted. Stay in contact through newsletters, invitations to appropriate events, such as an open house, and phone them just to say

'thanks'. Be sure to acknowledge milestones of five, 10, or 20 years of loyalty. All of these actions signal to your donors that they are valued.

29.   Survey your monthly donors to find out who they are and why they give. This is a cost-effective way to discover where to find good prospects – people who have similarities with your current supporters.

30.   Find out what motivates your donors to give monthly and incorporate these motivations into your recruitment campaigns.

31.   Be careful sending premiums (DVDs, mugs, or books) to donors once they are on a monthly giving programme. Some donors will love the gift, but others will resent you for spending their donation on anything other than your mission. A great option: get a board member, business, or a major donor to pay for the gift. Tell your donors that an individual (or a business) wanted to recognise their special role and generous donations with a gift. Emphasise that the monthly donor's gifts all go to support the mission.

32.   If you have a large programme, create a

specially tailored communication programme to recognise different interests, preferred methods of communication, longevity, or monthly giving level.

33. Develop an annual plan to recruit monthly donors. Involve all staff and volunteers. Make sure they know the great value of a successful programme.

34. Collecting gifts electronically saves a significant amount of money because processing an individual cheque is quite expensive, which diverts funds away from your mission.

35. Single gift or occasional donors who join a monthly giving programme will give an average of two to three times more per year than their previous annual amount.

36. The average monthly donor will probably give four to seven times more than the average single gift donor during any given year (not including donors who give $1,000 or more).

37. Organisations that are just starting a programme might have to educate their boards and staff about how EFT works. They might also have to explain how investing in building a programme brings long-term

income stability. Do your research and be prepared to answer questions.

38.   Always emphasise to donors, both in recruitment materials and in 'thank you' letters, that they can change or cancel their pledge at any time. This will eliminate a barrier for some people who might be hesitant to commit.

39.   Be sure to communicate clearly to your donors that EFT and credit card transactions are both safe and secure – and make sure you can back this up. Charities must be able to guarantee that their donors' financial information is completely protected.

40.   Once you have built up a group of committed donors, you should design a unique communication programme for them – one that is different from your regular donor communications and that recognises their special status.

41.   It is very important to have an effective and efficient 'back-end system'. This encompasses the management of donor communications and relationships, as well as gift processing technology.

42.   A superior donor management system will do more than just house a list of donors

or prospects. It will effectively handle the tasks related to collecting and analysing gifts. Some of the basic system functions include coding data, tracking histories, segmenting, personalising data, reporting and analysing.

43.   Educate yourself about EFT. The methods of collecting EFT gifts vary from country to country. For example, in Canada banks and credit unions provide this service at a reasonable cost, as do banks in Europe. In the US, there are a number of companies that facilitate the processing of EFT, credit card and direct debit transactions for a reasonable fee. These US companies can also provide charities with other services ranging from address changes to donor data reporting and analysis.

Epilogue

W ell it's been five years since I first met Helga at the call centre. And the encounter changed my life forever. Before her, I had been on a path where my only career option seemed to be getting a doctorate and trying to find a job somewhere as a philosophy professor. I know I would have made the subject interesting to students whose priority was dealing with their raging hormones, but let's face it: raising money is much more fun and – I'm delighted to report – much more emotionally rewarding.

So, I was saved from a life of threadbare tweed

jackets with elbow patches, paisley cravats and marking papers full of bad grammar. But, I still love philosophy and it comes in handy when my twins throw all their spaghetti on the floor and at each other. At these times, I am comforted by Aristotle, who said: 'For the things we have to learn before we can do them, we learn by doing them.' And throwing spaghetti around takes practice. My other favourite philosopher, Dave Barry, says, 'You can only be young once. But you can always be immature.'

Yes, I'm a dad now: a father of twins, busy with a three-day-a-week job as a fundraiser for PAWS. I care for the twins on the other two days while my wife is at work.

You know, being married makes the appeal of monthly giving so much clearer to me. Each month I pay for electricity, gas and the mortgage (isn't 30 too young to have a mortgage?), newspaper subscription, telephone and internet. And that's just for starters. The world seems to be conveniently organised to pay bills monthly. At least it's convenient for me. I can plan our family's finances because I know what's coming and when. Plus, my income comes in once a month to balance the expenditures.

And the income/expenditure schedule that virtually every adult has allows people to easily incorporate monthly pledges. Just as you would plan to pay your heating bill each month, you plan to 'pay' the charity – although the charity usually gets a lot less than the utility company.

I'm now on three monthly giving programmes: PAWS (of course), an AIDS charity (thanks to Tisa) and a children's charity. My wife gives to two groups: PAWS and the hospice where her grandmother died.

Five pledges per month really adds up and sometimes we are overdrawn at the bank. But do we consider dropping these monthly donations? Never – the money just automatically leaves our accounts, goes to the charities and we don't miss it. And the tax receipts do come in handy at the end of the year.

I suspect we'll be on these programmes for the rest of our lives. Almost certainly we'll start giving larger monthly amounts, once we become more financially secure, pay off our mortgage and the twins have completed university. At least until the kids move back in again, that is. But eventually they will leave and start their own lives, or so I've heard. Almost certainly by the time they are 40 and definitely by the time they hit 50.

As for asking Helga out for coffee, I never did work up the nerve. I was just too shy and she was too radiant. I still regret not having the courage to approach her. But today I am a happily married man with two beautiful children, Geoffrey and Alex. I have a nice, modest house and a meaningful job that I love.

Over the years I've studied human interaction (useful knowledge for every fundraiser) and I have discovered that in relationships women basically make all the decisions about choosing a partner. Lucky for me, I say.

You see, Helga actually asked me out for a coffee (a double half-fat caramel macchiato, if I remember correctly) and after hesitating for a few seconds – only because I was stunned – I said I'd love to.

Two years later we were married, in the woods, of course, which, as we discovered a little too late, is not amenable to high-heeled shoes (hers, not mine). The twins came pretty quickly afterwards and today they are going through the 'terrible twos'. I'm grateful on a daily basis for my philosophy training as I repeat to myself, 'this too shall pass'. I joke, of course, because they are the greatest thing that ever happened to me, or to Helga. They've made us even more dedicated to PAWS because we want them to grow up in a world with clean water, clean air, protected land and lots of wildlife. I believe we owe it to our children to do all we can to pass on to them a better world than the one we inherited.

You know, I'm glad I wrote this section because tomorrow I'm going to double my monthly gift to PAWS. And if you tell enough people about this book and they buy a copy, I'll be able to give a lot more to environmental causes. So let me ask you: will you tell three people about this book, say, on a monthly basis?

And let me thank you in advance for your generous support.

About the 'Tiny Essentials' series

The book you hold in your hands is part of a series of little books with a big mission. They focus on what really matters in one key area of voluntary sector management. Each book's purpose is to provide the essentials of its subject in an entertaining, easily digestible form, so people who otherwise wouldn't dream of reading a business book can effortlessly and enjoyably get access to what they really need to know.

Books in the 'Tiny Essentials' series are delightfully free of padding, waffle and over-blown theories. Extraneous material has been reduced to a minimum. Each book so lives up to its title that there's just no room for anything other than the essence of what really matters in the subject area, and how to order your priorities.

This 'Tiny' focuses on what every fundraiser, CEO and board member needs to know about establishing and developing a committed monthly giving programme. Other books in the 'Tiny' series are:

Tiny Essentials of Fundraising, by Neil Sloggie

Tiny Essentials of Writing for Fundraising, by George Smith

Tiny Essentials of Major Gift Fundraising, by Neil Sloggie

Tiny Essentials of an Effective Volunteer Board, by Ken Burnett

Tiny Essentials of Raising Money from Foundations and Trusts, by Jo Habib

All can be ordered at <u>www.whitelionpress.com</u>

A promise from
The White Lion Press

Enjoy the best books on fundraising and voluntary sector development.

Books by The White Lion Press will repay your investment many times over – and you'll enjoy reading them too. But if your purchase is damaged in any way, or if you feel any of our products do not live up to your expectations simply return them to us and we will issue you with a full refund, including any reasonable associated costs. We'll ask you to tell us why, so we can put right anything that might be wrong, but we won't quibble. Unfortunately we can only offer this if you bought the book directly from us, but even if you didn't, please let us know your problem and we'll do all we can to ensure your supplier matches our commitment to you. After all, you are our ultimate customer.

This guarantee applies to any books or videos you may purchase from us. We further promise to handle your orders with speed, efficiency and impressive politeness.

You can order further copies of this book, or any of our other titles, from our secure website, www.whitelionpress.com If you prefer, you can order by email, orders@whitelionpress.com; or fax, +33 (0)2 97 39 57 59; by post from Marie Burnett, The White Lion Press Limited, Kermarquer, 56310 Melrand, France, or by telephoning Marie on +33 (0)2 97 39 52 63.

All books are also available from www.amazon.co.uk

Tiny Essentials of Fundraising

by Neil Sloggie
Softback, 57 pp. ISBN 0-9518971-5-2

All you really need to know about fundraising, in one tiny book.

Join Kate, an inquisitive and ambitious new recruit to the fundraising profession, as she sets out to uncover what really matters in her chosen career by visiting and asking three seasoned practitioners. Like Kate you'll see as much to avoid as to emulate in the first two encounters but you'll be reassured and inspired as, in her final meeting, Kate discovers an organisation that has really thought through its fundraising strategy and approach, and shares with her – and you – the essential secrets of fundraising success.

'A simple and truthful reminder of what's at the heart of effective fundraising. How I wish someone had given me this book when I was starting out all those years ago!'
Jan Chisholm, managing director, Pareto Fundraising, Australia.

'I was given a copy of the "Tiny" book in Australia and was so enamoured of the clear message it conveys that I ordered a special edition to give to more than 1,500 fundraisers and all 700 Blackbaud employees. Their reactions have been universally positive. *Tiny Essentials of Fundraising* is one of those books that make us truly envious of the author for executing such a brilliant piece of writing...'
Robert Sywolski, chief executive, Blackbaud Inc, USA.

'It's a smart idea, well-executed – how fabulous to have a bite-sized book that sums up what makes for successful fundraising in such an accessible way to both native and non-native English speakers.

'Great stuff. Thanks Neil for what must be the shortest, simplest and yet very salient contribution to the world's literature on fundraising.'
Julie Weston, UNHCR, Switzerland.

Tiny Essentials of Writing for Fundraising

by George Smith
Softback, 65 pp.
ISBN 0-9518971-6-0

'I suggest your heart would soar if – once in a while – you received a letter written in decent English which said unexpected things in elegant ways, which moved you and stirred your emotions, which angered you or made you proud, a letter apparently written by one individual to another individual. For you never see these letters any more…'

If you believe that words matter then this opinionated little book is for you. For this 'Tiny' book will change forever the way you and your organisation communicate.

'*Tiny Essentials of Writing for Fundraising* is a refreshing – and delightfully short – guide to the author's insights about the writer's craft. If you're even thinking about writing fundraising letters you can't afford not to buy this remarkable little book.'
Mal Warwick, chairman, Mal Warwick & Associates Inc, USA.

'I am a huge fan of George's blunt but refined writing, his clear and individual voice, and his extraordinary ability to cut through the crap – keep this wonderful little book next to your pen and pc.'
Lyndall Stein, CEO, Concern, UK.

'Smith is a self-confessed curmudgeon but nobody describes better than he the power of words to advance your cause. The 11,149 words in this lovely book have been carefully selected and assembled to help you write well enough to convince anyone of anything.'
Ken Burnett, author, *Relationship Fundraising*; chairman, The Cascaid Group, UK.

Tiny Essentials of Major Gift Fundraising

by Neil Sloggie
Softback, 61 pp. ISBN 0-9518971-7-9

The natural successor to his first book, *Tiny Essentials of Fundraising*, this time Neil Sloggie tells the story of Daniel, who had never thought of asking any donor individually for money, nor of asking for more than a three-figure sum. Join him in his search to uncover the Holy Grail of major gift fundraising and learn as he did how to secure donations bigger than a house – and lots of them.

This 'Tiny' contains in their purest, most distilled form the priceless secrets of a neglected area of vast fundraising potential.

'Help is close at hand in this small gem – wise counsel, the importance of colleagues and networking, heaps of practical advice. To borrow Neil's words, "keep this one near the top of your priority pile".'
Sue-Anne Wallace, chief executive officer, Fundraising Institute-Australia.

'... a really helpful guide, especially to someone just starting out or wishing to do a quick reappraisal of their operation.'
Nick Booth, campaign director, NSPCC 'Full Stop' campaign, UK.

'... very accessible and conversational... a must for all those considering or involved in this form of fundraising.'
Maggie Taylor, consultant and trainer, UK.

Tiny Essentials of an Effective Volunteer Board

by Ken Burnett
Softback, 81 pp. ISBN 0-9518971-8-7

When Warren Maxwell is suddenly propelled into the chairman's seat of the voluntary organisation on whose board he serves, he decides that his somewhat mediocre board is going to become a paragon of all that's excellent in nonprofit governance. Join him on his brief, eventful, enlightening quest to discover what makes a balanced, progressive and highly effective volunteer board.

'This excellent and very readable book is essential for every board member of a charity. I realise how much better a chair and trustee I could have been if only the book had been written 30 years earlier.'
Lord Joel Joffe, former chair of trustees, Oxfam UK and chair, The Giving Campaign, UK.

'This tiny book is a huge contribution to the literature on governing boards. Told as a compelling story, the insights and experience-based facts are woven skilfully throughout. A delight to read, the lessons fly off the page.'
Kay Sprinkel Grace, author, *Beyond Fundraising* and *The Ultimate Board Member's Book*, USA.

'This energising, readable book draws out what's really important, the true "tiny essentials". The 21 keys summarised in chapter six are the cream on the cake…'
Noerine Kaleeba, chair of trustees, ActionAid International, South Africa.

'This little book is absolutely brilliant; it's easy to read and is full of useful information on how to improve the effectiveness of trustee boards.

'I found this book to be a very informative resource. I loved the style; to have a fictional story to read certainly drove home the salient points far more than a dull, factual text could have done and I found this approach to be very warm and engaging.'
Tracy Saunders, information officer, in *Volunteering Magazine* July 2006, UK.

'In every field there are those who become the "philosophers" of their fields. Burnett is such a philosopher for the field of fundraising. He is, in essence, a "guru".

'Burnett's new book is appropriate for his status as fundraising guru since it exhibits the wisdom and in-depth thinking that is characteristic of one who is steeped in the history, philosophy, and literature of the field.'
Joanne Fritz, in a review on the website Nonprofit Charitable Orgs (part of the New York Times Group) August 2006, USA.

Tiny Essentials of Raising Money from Foundations and Trusts

by Jo Habib
Softback, 77 pp.
ISBN 0-9518971-9-5

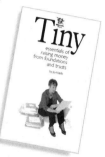

Of all the world's major donors (and they are major, giving away £33 billion plus each year in the UK and USA alone), foundations and trusts may be the most pure. They have no function other than to give their money away. In *Tiny Essentials of Raising Money from Foundations and Trusts*, Jo Habib shows you with precision how to get your share.

'This book brings clarity to a world that is often apparently obscure and will help anyone understand the steps that need to be taken when approaching others for money. Written clearly and simply it will be invaluable both to the novice and to experienced old hands who think they really understand their target market. It is definitely essential reading.'
Julia Unwin, consultant and author, *The Grant-Making Tango*, UK.

'This is an encyclopaedia on fundraising from foundations and trusts packed into a tiny book. Jo Habib covers everything a new fundraiser will need to know, with admirable clarity, thoroughness and authority. Experienced fundraisers should also refer to this splendid guide, using it as a check list against which to review their own practice.'
David Carrington, consultant, UK.

The Zen of Fundraising

by Ken Burnett
Published by Jossey-Bass Inc in
association with The White Lion Press
Limited. Softback, 169 pp. ISBN 978-0-
7879-8314-7

If all that has ever been said and written
about the art and science of fundraising
could be distilled down to just what
really matters there would be only a
small number of true gems deserving
of the description 'nuggets of information'.

Ken Burnett has identified and defined 89 such nuggets that he
presents here as *The Zen of Fundraising* – a fun-to-read, one-of-
a-kind look into what makes donors tick and, more importantly,
what makes them give.

'Ken Burnett knows what donors want and how fundraisers can
provide it. *The Zen of Fundraising* illustrates simple yet hard-earned
lessons through which fundraisers can engage their donors as real
partners, raising more money than ever. But to succeed, fundraisers
need to aspire to greater levels of communication and donor
engagement. This books shows us how.'
Chuck Longfield, founder and CEO, Target Software Inc, USA.

'The refreshingly brief principles provide inspiration and learning to
anyone striving for exceptional fundraising practice.'
Nicci Dent, director of fundraising, Médecins sans Frontières, Australia.

'A gentle blend of humour, personal experiences and practical
examples (but underpinned by pure steel), this book makes the
most compelling case yet for thinking about donor relationships.'
Adrian Sargeant, adjunct professor of philanthropy, Indiana University
Center on Philanthropy, USA.

Relationship Fundraising: A Donor-based Approach to the Business of Raising Money (second edition)

by Ken Burnett
Published by Jossey-Bass Inc in association with The White Lion Press Limited. Hardback, 384 pp. ISBN 0-7879-6089-6

Ken Burnett has completely revised and updated his classic book *Relationship Fundraising*. Filled with illustrative case examples, donor profiles, and more than 200 action points, this ground-breaking book shows fundraisers how to:

• Implement creative approaches to relationship-building fundraising.

• Avoid common fundraising errors and pitfalls.

• Apply the vital ingredients for fundraising success.

• Build good relationships with donors through marketing.

• Achieve a greater understanding of donors.

• Communicate effectively with donors – using direct mail, the press, television, the telephone, face-to-face contact, and more.

• Prepare for the challenges of twenty-first century fundraising.

'Not since Harold Seymour's classic, *Designs for Fund Raising*, has a book of this magnitude come along.

'Ken Burnett's updated and expanded work, *Relationship Fundraising*, just may be the book to which fundraising professionals turn for the next several decades.

'It is as brilliant as it is heartfelt, as simple as it is eloquent.'
Jerry Cianciolo, *The Compleat Professional's Library*, *Contributions Magazine*, USA.

'Ken Burnett's observations, insights and practical tips for building and sustaining relationships are superb. Highly readable, this book is a solid mix of sound theory and pragmatic application.'
Kay Sprinkel Grace, author, *Beyond Fund Raising*; co-author *High Impact Philanthropy*, USA.

'This is the book that sets the agenda for fundraising communications in the twenty-first century. Engaging, inspiring, and thought-provoking, *Relationship Fundraising* is based on the unique 25-year experience of one of the world's most respected fundraisers.'

Bernard Ross, director, The Management Centre, UK; co-author, *Breakthrough Thinking for Nonprofit Organizations*.

Friends for Life: Relationship Fundraising in Practice

by Ken Burnett
Hardback, 599 pp. ISBN 0-9518971-2-8

Amid the widespread acclaim that greeted the 1992 publication of Ken Burnett's *Relationship Fundraising* was one persistent qualified comment. Essentially the question was 'relationship fundraising sounds very attractive, but will it help us raise more money?'

In this accessible and entertaining sequel, Ken Burnett describes how relationship fundraising is working in a wide variety of organisations in the USA, Canada and the United Kingdom. Their stories provide the answer: a loud and resounding 'yes!'

But the ideas and experiences described in this book will do much more than just help fundraisers raise more money. They will show them how to develop and maintain strong, healthy, mutually beneficial relationships with their donors; relationships that will enable them to make friends for life.

The sequel to *Relationship Fundraising* first appeared in 1996, to international acclaim.

'I'm an enthusiastic fan of Ken Burnett's approach to building friends for life. His new book builds on the practical, common-sense approach to donor development he is famous for advocating.

'Great examples, an easy read – I highly recommend *Friends for*

Life: Relationship Fundraising in Practice.'
Dr Judith E Nichols, CFRE, author and consultant, USA.

'*Friends for Life* is a witty, readable tour of donor-think from both sides of the Atlantic and brings together a unique collection of experiences and anecdotes from many world-class fundraisers. *Relationship Fundraising* is already a classic throughout the world and this sequel is sure to have a similar impact.'
Jennie Thompson, consultant and co-founder of Craver, Mathews, Smith and Company, USA.

'The Botton Village case history is riveting. Its lessons have a relevance beyond fundraising. This is what direct marketing should always be, but so seldom is.'
Graeme McCorkell, author and consultant, UK.

Asking Properly: The Art of Creative Fundraising

by George Smith
Hardback, 220 pp.
ISBN 0-9518971-1-X

You will never read a book quite like this. George Smith tears open the conventional wisdom of fundraising creativity and so changes the rules for an entire trade. This book is irreverent, funny, savagely critical and genuinely inspiring, often on the same page.

Asking Properly is almost certainly the most authoritative book ever written about the creative aspects of fundraising. It is likely to remain a key text for years to come.

The author offers a profound analysis of donor motivation and is critical of the extent to which charities take their supporters for granted. But this book is no mere commentary on current practice – it offers a comprehensive checklist on how to optimise the creative presentation of the fundraising message. How to write, design, use direct mail, press advertising, broadcast media and the telephone, how to think in terms of fundraising products… the whole gallery of creativity and media is surveyed and assessed, with hundreds of examples of fundraising campaigns from around the world illustrating the need to 'ask properly'.

The book will prove invaluable to anyone involved in the fundraising process. It is provocative, entertaining and, above all, highly instructive. Read it, apply its lessons and it must enable you to raise more money.

'This book will become a classic. It's not just inspirational and a great read, there's a practical benefit on every page. When you apply George Smith's secrets you can hardly fail to improve your fundraising.'
Harvey McKinnon, president, Harvey McKinnon Associates, Canada.

'It's typically George Smith: wise, uncompromising, devastatingly critical of poor fundraising, brilliantly illustrative of what is good, full of ideas, funny, marvellously written – and exceptionally good value. In short, *Asking Properly* is one of those very few books you will keep for life.'
Pierre-Bernard Le Bas, head of fundraising, UNHCR, Switzerland.

Friends for Life video series

A series of half hour videos from the
Friends for Life sessions featuring Ken
Burnett in Vancouver, Canada in July
1996. Filmed by Canada's Knowledge
Network and produced jointly by
Harvey McKinnon Associates and The
White Lion Press.

Video One

• The challenge of relationship fundraising.

• How to introduce world-class donor service.

• Getting ahead of your competition.

Video Two

• Botton Village: the classic case history of superb relationship
fundraising.

• How you can profit from your donor's will.

• Four highly successful fundraising programmes.